A History Of Aeronautics
Part III

By

W. Lockwood Marsh And Evelyn Charles Vivian

A History of Aeronautics
Part III
by W. Lockwood Marsh And Evelyn Charles Vivian

ISBN: 978-93-62762-33-7

Published by

DOUBLE 9 BOOKS

2/13-B, Ansari Road
Daryaganj, New Delhi – 110002
info@double9books.com
www.double9books.com
Tel. 011-40042856

ABOUT THE AUTHOR

W. Lockwood Marsh and Evelyn Charles Vivian are distinguished authors renowned for their groundbreaking work, "A History of Aeronautics." This seminal masterpiece provides an exhaustive exploration of humanity's journey into the skies, tracing the evolution of flight from its earliest conceptualizations to the modern era of aviation. With meticulous research and captivating prose, Marsh and Vivian illuminate the pioneering efforts, technological advancements, and daring achievements that have shaped the field of aeronautics. Through comprehensive coverage of key milestones, groundbreaking inventions, and notable figures in aviation history, Marsh and Vivian offer readers a comprehensive understanding of the complex tapestry of human ingenuity and perseverance in conquering the skies. Their narrative skillfully navigates the intersection of science, technology, and human ambition, highlighting the triumphs and tribulations encountered in the pursuit of flight. "A History of Aeronautics" stands as a testament to Marsh and Vivian's dedication to chronicling the remarkable progress of aviation and its profound impact on society. This monumental work continues to inspire and inform aviation enthusiasts, historians, and scholars alike, ensuring its enduring legacy in the annals of aeronautical literature.

CONTENTS

FOREWORD

Although successful heavier-than-air flight is less than two decades old, and successful dirigible propulsion antedates it by a very short period, the mass of experiment and accomplishment renders any one-volume history of the subject a matter of selection. In addition to the restrictions imposed by space limits, the material for compilation is fragmentary, and, in many cases, scattered through periodical and other publications. Hitherto, there has been no attempt at furnishing a detailed account of how the aeroplane and the dirigible of to-day came to being, but each author who has treated the subject has devoted his attention to some special phase or section. The principal exception to this rule—Hildebrandt—wrote in 1906, and a good many of his statements are inaccurate, especially with regard to heavier-than-air experiment.

Such statements as are made in this work are, where possible, given with acknowledgment to the authorities on which they rest. Further acknowledgment is due to Lieut.-Col. Lockwood Marsh, not only for the section on aeroplane development which he has contributed to the work, but also for his kindly assistance and advice in connection with the section on aerostation. The author's thanks are also due to the Royal Aeronautical Society for free access to its valuable library of aeronautical literature, and to Mr A. Vincent Clarke for permission to make use of his notes on the development of the aero engine.

In this work is no claim to originality—it has been a matter mainly of compilation, and some stories, notably those of the Wright Brothers and of Santos Dumont, are better told in the words of the men themselves than any third party could tell them. The author claims, however, that this is the first attempt at recording the facts of development and stating, as fully as is possible in the compass of a single volume, how flight and aerostation have evolved. The time for a critical history of the subject is not yet.

In the matter of illustrations, it has been found very difficult to secure suitable material. Even the official series of photographs of aeroplanes in the war period is curiously incomplete' and the methods of censorship during that period prevented any complete series being privately collected. Omissions in this respect will probably be remedied in future editions of the work, as fresh material is constantly being located.

E.C.V. October, 1920.

PART III
AEROSTATICS

I
BEGINNINGS

Francesco Lana, with his 'aerial ship,' stands as one of the first great exponents of aerostatics; up to the time of the Montgolfier and Charles balloon experiments, aerostatic and aerodynamic research are so inextricably intermingled that it has been thought well to treat of them as one, and thus the work of Lana, Veranzio and his parachute, Guzman's frauds, and the like, have already been sketched. In connection with Guzman, Hildebrandt states in his Airships Past and Present, a fairly exhaustive treatise on the subject up to 1906, the year of its publication, that there were two inventors—or charlatans—Lorenzo de Guzman and a monk Bartolemeo Laurenzo, the former of whom constructed an unsuccessful airship out of a wooden basket covered with paper, while the latter made certain experiments with a machine of which no description remains. A third de Guzman, some twenty-five years later, announced that he had constructed a flying machine, with which he proposed to fly from a tower to prove his success to the public. The lack of record of any fatal accident overtaking him about that time seems to show that the experiment was not carried out.

Galien, a French monk, published a book L'art de naviguer dans l'air in 1757, in which it was conjectured that the air at high levels was lighter than that immediately over the surface of the earth. Galien proposed to bring down the upper layers of air and with them fill a vessel, which by Archimidean principle would rise through the heavier atmosphere. If one went high enough, said Galien, the air would be two thousand times as light as water, and it would be possible to construct an airship, with this light air as lifting factor, which should be as large as the town of Avignon, and carry four million passengers with their baggage. How this high air was to be obtained is matter for conjecture—Galien seems to have thought in a vicious circle, in which the vessel that must rise to obtain the light air must first be filled with it in order to rise.

Cavendish's discovery of hydrogen in 1776 set men thinking, and soon a certain Doctor Black was suggesting that vessels might be filled with hydrogen, in order that they might rise in the air. Black, however, did not get beyond suggestion; it was Leo Cavallo who first made experiments with hydrogen, beginning with filling soap bubbles, and passing on to bladders and special paper bags. In these latter the gas escaped, and Cavallo was about to try goldbeaters' skin at the time that the Montgolfiers came into the field with their hot air balloon.

Joseph and Stephen Montgolfier, sons of a wealthy French paper manufacturer, carried out many experiments in physics, and Joseph interested himself in the study of aeronautics some time before the first balloon was constructed by the brothers—he is said to have made a parachute descent from the roof of his house as early as 1771, but of this there is no proof. Galien's idea, together with study of the movement of clouds, gave Joseph some hope of achieving aerostation through Galien's schemes, and the first experiments were made by passing steam into a receiver, which, of course, tended to rise—but the rapid condensation of the steam prevented the receiver from more than threatening ascent. The experiments were continued with smoke, which produced only a slightly better effect, and, moreover, the paper bag into which the smoke was induced permitted of escape through its pores; finding this method a failure the brothers desisted until Priestley's work became known to them, and they conceived the use of hydrogen as a lifting factor. Trying this with paper bags, they found that the hydrogen escaped through the pores of the paper.

Their first balloon, made of paper, reverted to the hot-air principle; they lighted a fire of wool and wet straw under the balloon—and as a matter of course the balloon took fire after very little experiment; thereupon they constructed a second, having a capacity of 700 cubic feet, and this rose to a height of over 1,000 feet. Such a success gave them confidence, and they gave their first public exhibition on June 5th, 1783, with a balloon constructed of paper and of a circumference of 112 feet. A fire was lighted under this balloon, which, after rising to a height of 1,000 feet, descended through the cooling of the air inside a matter of ten minutes. At this the Academie des Sciences invited the brothers to conduct experiments in Paris.

The Montgolfiers were undoubtedly first to send up balloons, but other experimenters were not far behind them, and before they could get to Paris in response to their invitation, Charles, a prominent physicist of those days, had constructed a balloon of silk, which he proofed against escape of gas with rubber—the Roberts had just succeeded in dissolving this substance to permit of making a suitable coating for the silk. With a quarter of a ton of sulphuric acid, and half a ton of iron filings and turnings, sufficient hydrogen was generated in four days to fill Charles's balloon, which went up on August 28th, 1783. Although the day was wet, Paris turned out to the number of over 300,000 in the Champs de Mars, and cannon were fired to announce the ascent of the balloon. This, rising very rapidly, disappeared amid the rain clouds, but, probably bursting through no outlet being provided to compensate for the escape of gas, fell soon in the neighbourhood of Paris. Here peasants, ascribing evil supernatural influence to the fall of such a thing from nowhere, went at it with the implements of their craft— forks, hoes, and the like—and maltreated it severely, finally attaching it to a horse's tail and dragging it about until it was mere rag and scrap.

Meanwhile, Joseph Montgolfier, having come to Paris, set about the construction of a balloon out of linen; this was in three diverse sections, the top being a cone 30 feet in depth, the middle a cylinder 42 feet in diameter by 26 feet in depth, and the bottom another cone 20 feet in depth from junction with the cylindrical portion to its point. The balloon was both lined and covered with paper, decorated in blue and gold. Before ever an ascent could be attempted this ambitious balloon was caught in a heavy rainstorm which reduced its paper covering to pulp and tore the linen at its seams, so that a supervening strong wind tore the whole thing to shreds.

Montgolfier's next balloon was spherical, having a capacity of 52,000 cubic feet. It was made from waterproofed linen, and on September 19th, 1783, it made an ascent for the palace courtyard at Versailles, taking up as passengers a cock, a sheep, and a duck. A rent at the top of the balloon caused it to descend within eight minutes, and the duck and sheep were found none the worse for being the first living things to leave the earth in a balloon, but the cock, evidently suffering, was thought to have been affected by the rarefaction of the atmosphere at the tremendous height reached—for at that time the general opinion was that the atmosphere did not extend more than four or five miles above the earth's surface. It transpired later that the sheep had trampled on the cock, causing more solid injury than any that might be inflicted by rarefied air in an eight-minute ascent and descent of a balloon.

For achieving this flight Joseph Montgolfier received from the King of France a pension of of L40, while Stephen was given the order of St Michael, and a patent of nobility was granted to their father. They were made members of the Legion d'Honneur, and a scientific deputation, of which Faujas de Saint-Fond, who had raised the funds with which Charles's hydrogen balloon was constructed, presented to Stephen Montgolfier a gold medal struck in honour of his aerial conquest. Since Joseph appears to have had quite as much share in the success as Stephen, the presentation of the medal to one brother only was in questionable taste, unless it was intended to balance Joseph's pension.

Once aerostation had been proved possible, many people began the construction of small balloons—the wholehole thing was regarded as a matter of spectacles and a form of amusement by the great majority. A certain Baron de Beaumanoir made the first balloon of goldbeaters' skin, this being eighteen inches in diameter, and using hydrogen as a lifting factor. Few people saw any possibilities in aerostation, in spite of the adventures of the duck and sheep and cock; voyages to the moon were talked and written, and there was more of levity than seriousness over ballooning as a rule. The classic retort of Benjamin Franklin stands as an exception to the general rule: asked what was the use of ballooning—'What's the use of a baby?' he countered, and the spirit of that reply brought both the dirigible and the aeroplane to being, later.

The next noteworthy balloon was one by Stephen Montgolfier, designed to take up passengers, and therefore of rather large dimensions, as these things went then. The capacity was 100,000 cubic feet, the depth being 85 feet, and the exterior was very gaily decorated. A short, cylindrical opening was made at the lower extremity, and under this a fire-pan was suspended, above the passenger car of the balloon. On October 15th, 1783, Pilatre de Rozier made the first balloon ascent—but the balloon was held captive, and only allowed to rise to a height of 80 feet. But, a little later in 1783, Rozier secured the honour of making the first ascent in a free balloon, taking up with him the Marquis d'Arlandes. It had been originally intended that two criminals, condemned to death, should risk their lives in the perilous venture, with the prospect of a free pardon if they made a safe descent, but d'Arlandes got the royal consent to accompany Rozier, and the criminals lost their chance. Rozier and d'Arlandes made a voyage lasting for twenty-five minutes, and, on landing, the balloon collapsed with such rapidity as almost to suffocate Rozier, who, however, was dragged out to safety by d'Arlandes. This first aerostatic journey took place on November 21st, 1783.

Some seven months later, on June 4th, 1784, a Madame Thible ascended in a free balloon, reaching a height of 9,000 feet, and making a journey which lasted for forty-five minutes—the great King Gustavus of Sweden witnessed this ascent. France grew used to balloon ascents in the course of a few months, in spite of the brewing of such a storm as might have been calculated to wipe out all but purely political interests. Meanwhile, interest in the new discovery spread across the Channel, and on September 15th, 1784, one Vincent Lunardi made the first balloon voyage in England, starting from the Artillery Ground at Chelsea, with a cat and dog as passengers, and landing in a field in the parish of Standon, near Ware. There is a rather rare book which gives a very detailed account of this first ascent in England, one copy of which is in the library of the Royal Aeronautical Society; the venturesome Lunardi won a greater measure of fame through his exploit than did Cody for his infinitely more courageous and—from a scientific point of view—valuable first aeroplane ascent in this country.

The Montgolfier type of balloon, depending on hot air for its lifting power, was soon realised as having dangerous limitations. There was always a possibility of the balloon catching fire while it was being filled, and on landing there was further danger from the hot pan which kept up the supply of hot air on the voyage—the collapsing balloon fell on the pan, inevitably. The scientist Saussure, observing the filling of the balloons very carefully, ascertained that it was rarefaction of the air which was responsible for the lifting power, and not the heat in itself, and, owing to the rarefaction of the air at normal temperature at great heights above the earth, the limit of ascent for a balloon of the Montgolfier type was estimated by him at under 9,000 feet. Moreover, since the amount of fuel that could be carried for maintaining the heat of the balloon after inflation was subject to definite limits, prescribed by the carrying capacity of the balloon, the duration of the journey was necessarily limited just as strictly.

These considerations tended to turn the minds of those interested in aerostation to consideration of the hydrogen balloon evolved by Professor Charles. Certain improvements had been made by Charles since his first construction; he employed rubber-coated silk in the construction of a balloon of 30 feet diameter, and provided a net for distributing the pressure uniformly over the surface of the envelope; this net covered the top half of the balloon, and from its lower edge dependent ropes hung to join on a wooden ring, from which the car of the balloon was suspended—apart from the extension of the net so as to cover in the whole of the envelope, the spherical balloon of to-day is virtually identical with that of Charles in its method of construction. He introduced the valve at the top of the balloon, by which escape of gas could be controlled, operating his valve by means of ropes which depended to the car of the balloon, and he also inserted a tube, of about 7 inches diameter, at the bottom of the balloon, not only for purposes of inflation, but also to provide a means of escape for gas in case of expansion due to atmospheric conditions.

Sulphuric acid and iron filings were used by Charles for filling his balloon, which required three days and three nights for the generation of its 14,000 cubic feet of hydrogen gas. The inflation was completed on December 1st, 1783, and the fittings carried included a barometer and a grapnel form of anchor. In addition to this, Charles provided the first 'ballon sonde' in the form of a small pilot balloon which he handed to Montgolfier to launch before his own ascent, in order to determine the direction and velocity of the wind. It was a graceful compliment to his rival, and indicated that, although they were both working to the one end, their rivalry was not a matter of bitterness.

Ascending on December 1st, 1783, Charles took with him one of the brothers Robert, and with him made the record journey up to that date, covering a period of three and three-quarter hours, in which time they journeyed some forty miles. Robert then landed, and Charles ascended again alone, reaching such a height as to feel the effects of the rarefaction of the air, this very largely due to the rapidity of his ascent. Opening the valve at the top of the balloon, he descended thirty-five minutes after leaving Robert behind, and came to earth a few miles from the point of the first descent. His discomfort over the rapid ascent was mainly due to the fact that, when Robert landed, he forgot to compensate for the reduction of weight by taking in further ballast, but the ascent proved the value of the tube at the bottom of the balloon envelope, for the gas escaped very rapidly in that second ascent, and, but for the tube, the balloon must inevitably have burst in the air, with fatal results for Charles.

As in the case of aeroplane flight, as soon as the balloon was proved practicable the flight across the English Channel was talked of, and Rozier, who had the honour of the first flight, announced his intention of being first to cross. But Blanchard, who had an idea for a 'flying car,' anticipated him, and made a start from Dover on January 7th, 1785, taking with him an American doctor named Jeffries. Blanchard fitted out his craft for the journey very thoroughly, taking provisions, oars, and even wings, for propulsion in case of need. He took so much, in fact, that as soon as the balloon lifted clear of the ground the whole of the ballast had to be jettisoned, lest the balloon should drop into the sea. Half-way across the Channel the sinking of the balloon warned Blanchard that he had to part with more than ballast to accomplish the journey, and all the equipment went, together with certain books and papers that were on board the car. The balloon looked perilously like collapsing, and both Blanchard and Jeffries began to undress in order further to lighten their craft—Jeffries even proposed a heroic dive to save the situation, but suddenly the balloon rose sufficiently to clear the French coast, and the two voyagers landed at a point near Calais in the Forest of Gaines, where a marble column was subsequently erected to commemorate the great feat.

Rozier, although not first across, determined to be second, and for that purpose he constructed a balloon which was to owe its buoyancy to a combination of the hydrogen and hot air principles. There was a spherical hydrogen balloon above, and beneath it a cylindrical container which could be filled with hot air, thus compensating for the leakage of gas from the hydrogen portion of the balloon—regulating the heat of his fire, he thought, would give him perfect control in the matter of ascending and descending.

On July 6th, 1785, a favourable breeze gave Rozier his opportunity of starting from the French coast, and with a passenger aboard he cast off in his balloon, which he had named the 'Aero-Montgolfiere.' There was a rapid rise at first, and then for a time the balloon remained stationary over the land, after which a cloud suddenly appeared round the balloon, denoting that an explosion had taken place. Both Rozier and his companion were killed in the fall, so that he, first to leave the earth by balloon, was also first victim to the art of aerostation.

There followed, naturally, a lull in the enthusiasm with which ballooning had been taken up, so far as France was concerned. In Italy, however, Count Zambeccari took up hot-air ballooning, using a spirit lamp to give him buoyancy, and on the first occasion when the balloon car was set on fire Zambeccari let down his passenger by means of the anchor rope, and managed to extinguish the fire while in the air. This reduced the buoyancy of the balloon to such an extent that it fell into the Adriatic and was totally wrecked, Zambeccari being rescued by fishermen. He continued to experiment up to 1812, when he attempted to ascend at Bologna; the spirit in his lamp was upset by the collision of the car with a tree, and the car was again set on fire. Zambeccari jumped from the car when it was over fifty feet above level ground, and was killed. With him the Rozier type of balloon, combining the hydrogen and hot air principles, disappeared; the combination was obviously too dangerous to be practical.

The brothers Robert were first to note how the heat of the sun acted on the gases within a balloon envelope, and it has since been ascertained that sun rays will heat the gas in a balloon to as much as 80 degrees Fahrenheit greater temperature than the surrounding atmosphere; hydrogen, being less affected by change of temperature than coal gas, is the most suitable filling element, and coal gas comes next as the medium of buoyancy. This for the free and non-navigable balloon, though for the airship, carrying means of combustion, and in military work liable to ignition by explosives, the gas helium seems likely to replace hydrogen, being non-combustible.

In spite of the development of the dirigible airship, there remains work for the free, spherical type of balloon in the scientific field. Blanchard's companion on the first Channel crossing by balloon, Dr Jeffries, was the first balloonist to ascend for purely scientific purposes; as early as 1784 he made an ascent to a height of 9,000 feet, and observed a fall in temperature of from degrees—at the level of London, where he began his ascent—to 29 degrees at the maximum height reached. He took up an electrometer, a hydrometer, a compass, a thermometer, and a Toricelli barometer, together with bottles of water, in order to collect samples of the air at different heights. In 1785 he made a second ascent, when trigonometrical observations of the height of the balloon were made from the French coast, giving an altitude of 4,800 feet.

The matter was taken up on its scientific side very early in America, experiments in Philadelphia being almost simultaneous with those of the Montgolfiers in France. The flight of Rozier and d'Arlandes inspired two members of the Philadelphia Philosophical Academy to construct a balloon or series of balloons of their own design; they made a machine which consisted of no less than 47 small hydrogen balloons attached to a wicker car, and made certain preliminary trials, using animals as passengers. This was followed by a captive ascent with a man as passenger, and eventually by the first free ascent in America, which was undertaken by one James Wilcox, a carpenter, on December 28th, 1783. Wilcox, fearful of falling into a river, attempted to regulate his landing by cutting slits in some of the supporting balloons, which was the method adopted for regulating ascent or descent in this machine. He first cut three, and then, finding that the effect produced was not sufficient, cut three more, and then another five—eleven out of the forty-seven. The result was so swift a descent that he dislocated his wrist on landing.

A NOTE ON BALLONETS OR AIR BAGS.

Meusnier, toward the end of the eighteenth century, was first to conceive the idea of compensating for the loss of gas due to expansion by fitting to the interior of a free balloon a ballonet, or air bag, which could be pumped full of air so as to retain the shape and rigidity of the envelope.

The ballonet became particularly valuable as soon as airship construction became general, and it was in the course of advance in Astra Torres design that the project was introduced of using the ballonets in order to give inclination from the horizontal. In the earlier Astra Torres, trimming was accomplished by moving the car fore and aft—this in itself was an advance on the separate 'sliding weigh' principle—and this was the method followed in the Astra Torres bought by the British Government from France in 1912 for training airship pilots. Subsequently, the two ballonets fitted inside the envelope were made to serve for trimming by the extent of their inflation, and this method of securing inclination proved the best until exterior rudders, and greater engine power, supplanted it, as in the Zeppelin and, in fact, all rigid types.

In the kite balloon, the ballonet serves the purpose of a rudder, filling itself through the opening being kept pointed toward the wind—there is an ingenious type of air scoop with non-return valve which assures perfect inflation. In the S.S. type of airship, two ballonets are provided, the supply of air being taken from the propeller draught by a slanting aluminium tube to the underside of the envelope, where it meets a longitudinal fabric hose which connects the two ballonet air inlets. In this hose the non-return air valves, known as 'crab-pots,' are fitted, on either side of the junction with the air-scoop. Two automatic air valves, one for each ballonet, are fitted in the underside of the envelope, and, as the air pressure tends to open these instead of keeping them shut, the spring of the valve is set inside the envelope. Each spring is set to open at a pressure of 25 to 28 mm.

II
THE FIRST DIRIGIBLES

Having got off the earth, the very early balloonists set about the task of finding a means of navigating the air but, lacking steam or other accessory power to human muscle, they failed to solve the problem. Joseph Montgolfier speedily exploded the idea of propelling a balloon either by means of oars or sails, pointing out that even in a dead calm a speed of five miles an hour would be the limit achieved. Still, sailing balloons were constructed, even up to the time of Andree, the explorer, who proposed to retard the speed of the balloon by ropes dragging on the ground, and then to spread a sail which should catch the wind and permit of deviation of the course. It has been proved that slight divergences from the course of the wind can be obtained by this means, but no real navigation of the air could be thus accomplished.

Professor Wellner, of Brunn, brought up the idea of a sailing balloon in more practical fashion in 1883. He observed that surfaces inclined to the horizontal have a slight lateral motion in rising and falling, and deduced that by alternate lowering and raising of such surfaces he would be able to navigate the air, regulating ascent and descent by increasing or decreasing the temperature of his buoyant medium in the balloon. He calculated that a balloon, 50 feet in diameter and 150 feet in length, with a vertical surface in front and a horizontal surface behind, might be navigated at a speed of ten miles per hour, and in actual tests at Brunn he proved that a single rise and fall moved the balloon three miles against the wind. His ideas were further developed by Lebaudy in the construction of the early French dirigibles.

According to Hildebrandt,[*] the first sailing balloon was built in 1784 by Guyot, who made his balloon egg-shaped, with the smaller end at the back and the longer axis horizontal; oars were intended to propel the craft, and naturally it was a failure. Carra proposed the use of paddle wheels, a step in the right direction, by mounting them on the sides of the car, but the improvement was only slight. Guyton de Morveau, entrusted by the Academy of Dijon with the building of a sailing balloon, first used a vertical rudder at the rear end of his construction—it survives in the modern dirigible. His construction included sails and oars, but, lacking steam or other than human propulsive power, the airship was a failure equally with Guyot's.

[*] Airships Past and Present.

Two priests, Miollan and Janinet, proposed to drive balloons through the air by the forcible expulsion of the hot air in the envelope from the rear of the balloon. An opening was made about half-way up the envelope, through which the hot air was to escape, buoyancy being maintained by a pan of combustibles in the car. Unfortunately, this development of the Montgolfier type never got a trial, for those who were to be spectators of the first flight grew exasperated at successive delays, and in the end, thinking that the balloon would never rise, they destroyed it.

Meusnier, a French general, first conceived the idea of compensating for loss of gas by carrying an air bag inside the balloon, in order to maintain the full expansion of the envelope. The brothers Robert constructed the first balloon in which this was tried and placed the air bag near the neck of the balloon which was intended to be driven by oars, and steered by a rudder. A violent swirl of wind which was encountered on the first ascent tore away the oars and rudder and broke the ropes which held the air bag in position; the bag fell into the opening of the neck and stopped it up, preventing the escape of gas under expansion. The Duc de Chartres, who was aboard, realised the extreme danger of the envelope bursting as the balloon ascended, and at 16,000 feet he thrust a staff through the envelope— another account says that he slit it with his sword—and thus prevented disaster. The descent after this rip in the fabric was swift, but the passengers got off without injury in the landing.

Meusnier, experimenting in various ways, experimented with regard to the resistance offered by various shapes to the air, and found that an elliptical shape was best; he proposed to make the car boat—shaped, in order further to decrease the resistance, and he advocated an entirely rigid connection between the car and the body of the balloon, as indispensable to a dirigible.[*] He suggested using three propellers, which were to be driven by hand by means of pulleys, and calculated that a crew of eighty would be required to furnish sufficient motive power. Horizontal fins were to be used to assure stability, and Meusnier thoroughly investigated the pressures exerted by gases, in order to ascertain the stresses to which the envelope would be subjected. More important still, he went into detail with regard to the use of air bags, in order to retain the shape of the balloon under varying pressures of gas due to expansion and consequent losses; he proposed two separate envelopes, the inner one containing gas, and the space between it and the outer one being filled with air. Further, by compressing the air inside the air bag, the rate of ascent or descent could be regulated. Lebaudy, acting on this principle, found it possible to pump air at the rate of 35 cubic feet per second, thus making good loss of ballast which had to be thrown overboard.

[*] Hildebrandt.

Meusnier's balloon, of course, was never constructed, but his ideas have been of value to aerostation up to the present time. His career ended in the revolutionary army in 1793, when he was killed in the fighting before Mayence, and the King of Prussia ordered all firing to cease until Meusnier had been buried. No other genius came forward to carry on his work, and it was realised that human muscle could not drive a balloon with certainty through the air; experiment in this direction was abandoned for nearly sixty years, until in 1852 Giffard brought the first practicable power-driven dirigible to being.

Giffard, inventor of the steam injector, had already made balloon ascents when he turned to aeronautical propulsion, and constructed a steam engine of 5 horsepower with a weight of only 100 lbs.—a great achievement for his day. Having got his engine, he set about making the balloon which it was to drive; this he built with the aid of two other enthusiasts, diverging from Meusnier's ideas by making the ends pointed, and keeping the body narrowed from Meusnier's ellipse to a shape more resembling a rather fat cigar. The length was 144 feet, and the greatest diameter only 40 feet, while the capacity was 88,000 cubic feet. A net which covered the envelope of the balloon supported a spar, 66 feet in length, at the end of which a triangular sail was placed vertically to act as rudder. The car, slung 20 feet below the spar, carried the engine and propeller. Engine and boiler together weighed 350 lbs., and drove the 11 foot propeller at 110 revolutions per minute.

As precaution against explosion, Giffard arranged wire gauze in front of the stoke-hole of his boiler, and provided an exhaust pipe which discharged the waste gases from the engine in a downward direction. With this first dirigible he attained to a speed of between 6 and 8 feet per second, thus proving that the propulsion of a balloon was a possibility, now that steam had come to supplement human effort.

Three years later he built a second dirigible, reducing the diameter and increasing the length of the gas envelope, with a view to reducing air resistance. The length of this was 230 feet, the diameter only 33 feet, and the capacity was 113,000 cubic feet, while the upper part of the envelope, to which the covering net was attached, was specially covered to ensure a stiffening effect. The car of this dirigible was dropped rather lower than that of the first machine, in order to provide more thoroughly against the danger of explosions. Giffard, with a companion named Yon as passenger, took a trial trip on this vessel, and made a journey against the wind, though slowly. In commencing to descend, the nose of the envelope tilted upwards, and the weight of the car and its contents caused the net to slip, so that just before the dirigible reached the ground, the envelope burst. Both Giffard and his companion escaped with very slight injuries.

Plans were immediately made for the construction of a third dirigible, which was to be 1,970 feet in length, 98 feet in extreme diameter, and to have a capacity of 7,800,000 cubic feet of gas. The engine of this giant was to have weighed 30 tons, and with it Giffard expected to attain a speed of 40 miles per hour. Cost prevented the scheme being carried out, and Giffard went on designing small steam engines until his invention of the steam injector gave him the funds to turn to dirigibles again. He built a captive balloon for the great exhibition in London in 1868, at a cost of nearly L30,000, and designed a dirigible balloon which was to have held a million and three quarters cubic feet of gas, carry two boilers, and cost about L40,000. The plans were thoroughly worked out, down to the last detail, but the dirigible was never constructed. Giffard went blind, and died in 1882—he stands as the great pioneer of dirigible construction, more on the strength of the two vessels which he actually built than on that of the ambitious later conceptions of his brain.

In 1872 Dupuy de Lome, commissioned by the French government, built a dirigible which he proposed to drive by man-power—it was anticipated that the vessel would be of use in the siege of Paris, but it was not actually tested till after the conclusion of the war. The length of this vessel was 118 feet, its greatest diameter 49 feet, the ends being pointed, and the motive power was by a propeller which was revolved by the efforts of eight men. The vessel attained to about the same speed as Giffard's steam-driven airship; it was capable of carrying fourteen men, who, apart from these engaged in driving the propeller, had to manipulate the pumps which controlled the air bags inside the gas envelope.

In the same year Paul Haenlein, working in Vienna, produced an airship which was a direct forerunner of the Lebaudy type, 164 feet in length, 30 feet greatest diameter, and with a cubic capacity of 85,000 feet. Semi-rigidity was attained by placing the car as close to the envelope as possible, suspending it by crossed ropes, and the motive power was a gas engine of the Lenoir type, having four horizontal cylinders, and giving about 5 horse-power with a consumption of about 250 cubic feet of gas per hour. This gas was sucked from the envelope of the balloon, which was kept fully inflated by pumping in compensating air to the air bags inside the main envelope. A propeller, 15 feet in diameter, was driven by the Lenoir engine at 40 revolutions per minute. This was the first instance of the use of an internal combustion engine in connection with aeronautical experiments.

The envelope of this dirigible was rendered airtight by means of internal rubber coating, with a thinner film on the outside. Coal gas, used for inflation, formed a suitable fuel for the engine, but limited the height to which the dirigible could ascend. Such trials as were made were carried out with the dirigible held captive, and a speed of I 5 feet per second was attained. Full experiment was prevented through funds running low, but Haenlein's work constituted a distinct advance on all that had been done previously.

Two brothers, Albert and Gaston Tissandier, were next to enter the field of dirigible construction; they had experimented with balloons during the Franc-Prussian War, and had attempted to get into Paris by balloon during the siege, but it was not until 1882 that they produced their dirigible.

This was 92 feet in length and 32 feet in greatest diameter, with a cubic capacity of 37,500 feet, and the fabric used was varnished cambric. The car was made of bamboo rods, and in addition to its crew of three, it carried a Siemens dynamo, with 24 bichromate cells, each of which weighed 17 lbs. The motor gave out 1 1/2 horse-power, which was sufficient to drive the vessel at a speed of up to 10 feet per second. This was not so good as Haenlein's previous attempt and, after L2,000 had been spent, the Tissandier abandoned their experiments, since a 5-mile breeze was sufficient to nullify the power of the motor.

Renard, a French officer who had studied the problem of dirigible construction since 1878, associated himself first with a brother officer named

La Haye, and subsequently with another officer, Krebs, in the construction of the second dirigible to be electrically-propelled. La Haye first approached Colonel Laussedat, in charge of the Engineers of the French Army, with a view to obtaining funds, but was refused, in consequence of the practical failure of all experiments since 1870. Renard, with whom Krebs had now associated himself, thereupon went to Gambetta, and succeeded in getting a promise of a grant of L8,000 for the work; with this promise Renard and Krebs set to work.

They built their airship in torpedo shape, 165 feet in length, and of just over 27 feet greatest diameter—the greatest diameter was at the front, and the cubic capacity was 66,000 feet. The car itself was 108 feet in length, and 4 1/2 feet broad, covered with silk over the bamboo framework. The 23 foot diameter propeller was of wood, and was driven by an electric motor connected to an accumulator, and yielding 8.5 horsepower. The sweep of the propeller, which might have brought it in contact with the ground in landing, was counteracted by rendering it possible to raise the axis on which the blades were mounted, and a guide rope was used to obviate damage altogether, in case of rapid descent. There was also a 'sliding weight' which was movable to any required position to shift the centre of gravity as desired. Altogether, with passengers and ballast aboard, the craft weighed two tons.

In the afternoon of August 8th, 1884, Renard and Krebs ascended in the dirigible—which they had named 'La France,' from the military ballooning ground at Chalais-Meudon, making a circular flight of about five miles, the latter part of which was in the face of a slight wind. They found that the vessel answered well to her rudder, and the five-mile flight was made successfully in a period of 23 minutes. Subsequent experimental flights determined that the air speed of the dirigible was no less than 14 1/2 miles per hour, by far the best that had so far been accomplished in dirigible flight. Seven flights in all were made, and of these five were completely successful, the dirigible returning to its starting point with no difficulty. On the other two flights it had to be towed back.

Renard attempted to repeat his construction on a larger scale, but funds would not permit, and the type was abandoned; the motive power was not sufficient to permit of more than short flights, and even to the present time electric motors, with their necessary accumulators, are far too cumbrous to compete with the self-contained internal combustion engine. France had to wait for the Lebaudy brothers, just as Germany had to wait for Zeppelin and Parseval.

Two German experimenters, Baumgarten and Wolfert, fitted a Daimler motor to a dirigible balloon which made its first ascent at Leipzig in 1880. This vessel had three cars, and placing a passenger in one of the outer cars[*] distributed the load unevenly, so that the whole vessel tilted over and crashed to the earth, the occupants luckily escaping without injury. After Baumgarten's death, Wolfert determined to carry on with his experiments, and, having achieved a certain measure of success, he announced an ascent to take place on the Tempelhofer Field, near Berlin, on June 12th, 1897. The vessel, travelling with the wind, reached a height of 600 feet, when the exhaust of the motor communicated flame to the envelope of the balloon, and Wolfert, together with a passenger he carried, was either killed by the fall or burnt to death on the ground. Giffard had taken special precautions to avoid an accident of this nature, and Wolfert, failing to observe equal care, paid the full penalty.

[*] Hildebrandt.

Platz, a German soldier, attempting an ascent on the Tempelhofer Field in the Schwartz airship in 1897, merely proved the dirigible a failure. The vessel was of aluminium, 0.008 inch in thickness, strengthened by an aluminium lattice work; the motor was two-cylindered petrol-driven; at the first trial the metal developed such leaks that the vessel came to the ground within four miles of its starting point. Platz, who was aboard alone as crew, succeeded in escaping by jumping clear before the car touched earth, but the shock of alighting broke up the balloon, and a following high wind completed the work of full destruction. A second account says that Platz, finding the propellers insufficient to drive the vessel against the wind, opened the valve and descended too rapidly.

The envelope of this dirigible was 156 feet in length, and the method of filling was that of pushing in bags, fill them with gas, and then pulling them to pieces and tearing them out of the body of the balloon. A second contemplated method of filling was by placing a linen envelope inside the aluminium casing, blowing it out with air, and then admitting the gas between the linen and the aluminium outer casing. This would compress the air out of the linen envelope, which was to be withdrawn when the aluminium casing had been completely filled with gas.

All this, however, assumes that the Schwartz type—the first rigid dirigible, by the way—would prove successful. As it proved a failure on the first trial, the problem of filling it did not arise again.

By this time Zeppelin, retired from the German army, had begun to devote himself to the study of dirigible construction, and, a year after Schwartz had made his experiment and had failed, he got together sufficient funds for the formation of a limitedliability company, and started on the construction of the first of his series of airships. The age of tentative experiment was over, and, forerunner of the success of the heavier-than-air type of flying machine, successful dirigible flight was accomplished by Zeppelin in Germany, and by Santos-Dumont in France.

III
SANTOS-DUMONT

A Brazilian by birth, Santos-Dumont began in Paris in the year 1898 to make history, which he subsequently wrote. His book, My Airships, is a record of his eight years of work on lighter-than-air machines, a period in which he constructed no less than fourteen dirigible balloons, beginning with a cubic capacity of 6,350 feet, and an engine of 3 horse-power, and rising to a cubic capacity of 71,000 feet on the tenth dirigible he constructed, and an engine of 60 horse-power, which was fitted to the seventh machine in order of construction, the one which he built after winning the Deutsch Prize.

The student of dirigible construction is recommended to Santos-Dumont's own book not only as a full record of his work, but also as one of the best stories of aerial navigation that has ever been written. Throughout all his experiments, he adhered to the non-rigid type; his first dirigible made its first flight on September 18th, 1898, starting from the Jardin d'Acclimatation to the west of Paris; he calculated that his 3 horse-power engine would yield sufficient power to enable him to steer clear of the trees with which the starting-point was surrounded, but, yielding to the advice of professional aeronauts who were present, with regard to the placing of the dirigible for his start, he tore the envelope against the trees. Two days later, having repaired the balloon, he made an ascent of 1,300 feet. In descending, the hydrogen left in the balloon contracted, and Santos-Dumont narrowly escaped a serious accident in coming to the ground.

His second machine, built in the early spring of 1899, held over 7,000 cubic feet of gas and gave a further 44 lbs. of ascensional force. The balloon envelope was very long and very narrow; the first attempt at flight was made in wind and rain, and the weather caused sufficient contraction of the hydrogen for a wind gust to double the machine up and toss it into the trees near its starting-point. The inventor immediately set about the construction of 'Santos-Dumont No. 3,' on which he made a number of successful flights, beginning on November 13th, 1899. On the last of his flights, he lost the rudder of the machine and made a fortunate landing at Ivry. He did not repair the balloon, considering it too clumsy in form and its motor too small.

Consequently No. 4 was constructed, being finished on the 1st, August, 1900. It had a cubic capacity of 14,800 feet, a length of 129 feet and greatest diameter of 16.7 feet, the power plant being a 7 horse-power Buchet motor. Santos-Dumont sat on a bicycle saddle fixed to the long bar suspended under the machine, which also supported motor propeller, ballast; and fuel. The experiment of placing the propeller at the stem instead of at the stern was tried, and the motor gave it a speed of 100 revolutions per minute. Professor Langley witnessed the trials of the machine, which proved before the members of the International Congress of Aeronautics, on September 19th, that it was capable of holding its own against a strong wind.

Finding that the cords with which his dirigible balloon cars were suspended offered almost as much resistance to the air as did the balloon itself, Santos-Dumont substituted piano wire and found that the alteration constituted greater progress than many a more showy device. He altered the shape and size of his No. 4 to a certain extent and fitted a motor of 12 horse-power. Gravity was controlled by shifting weights worked by a cord; rudder and propeller were both placed at the stern. In Santos-Dumont's book there is a certain amount of confusion between the No. 4 and No. 5 airships, until he explains that 'No. 5' is the reconstructed 'No. 4.' It was with No. 5 that he won the Encouragement Prize presented by the Scientific Commission of the Paris Aero Club. This he devoted to the first aeronaut who between May and October of 1900 should start from St Cloud, round the Eiffel Tower, and return. If not won in that year, the prize was to remain open the following year from May 1st to October 1st, and so on annually until won. This was a simplification of the conditions of the Deutsch Prize itself, the winning of which involved a journey of 11 kilometres in 30 minutes.

The Santos-Dumont No. 5, which was in reality the modified No. 4 with new keel, motor, and propeller, did the course of the Deutsch Prize, but with it Santos-Dumont made no attempt to win the prize until July of 1901, when he completed the course in 40 minutes, but tore his balloon in landing. On the 8th August, with his balloon leaking, he made a second attempt, and narrowly escaped disaster, the airship being entirely wrecked. Thereupon he built No. 6 with a cubic capacity of 22,239 feet and a lifting power of 1,518 lbs.

With this machine he won the Deutsch Prize on October 19th, 1901, starting with the disadvantage of a side wind of 20 feet per second. He reached the Eiffel Tower in 9 minutes and, through miscalculating his turn, only just missed colliding with it. He got No. 6 under control again and succeeded in getting back to his starting-point in 29 1/2 minutes, thus winning the 125,000 francs which constituted the Deutsch Prize, together with a similar sum granted to him by the Brazilian Government for the exploit. The greater part of this money was given by Santos-Dumont to charities.

He went on building after this until he had made fourteen non-rigid dirigibles; of these No. 12 was placed at the disposal of the military authorities, while the rest, except for one that was sold to an American and made only one trip, were matters of experiment for their maker. His conclusions from his experiments may be gathered from his own work:—

'On Friday, 31st July, 1903, Commandant Hirschauer and Lieutenant-Colonel Bourdeaux spent the afternoon with me at my airship station at Neuilly St James, where I had my three newest airships—the racing 'No. 7,' the omnibus 'No. 10,' and the runabout 'No. 9'—ready for their study. Briefly, I may say that the opinions expressed by the representatives of the Minister of War were so unreservedly favourable that a practical test of a novel character was decided to be made. Should the airship chosen pass successfully through it the result will be conclusive of its military value.

'Now that these particular experiments are leaving my exclusively private control I will say no more of them than what has been already published in the French press. The test will probably consist of an attempt to enter one of the French frontier towns, such as Belfort or Nancy, on the same day that the airship leaves Paris. It will not, of course, be necessary to make the whole journey in the airship. A military railway wagon may be assigned to carry it, with its balloon uninflated, with tubes of hydrogen to fill it, and with all the necessary machinery and instruments arranged beside it. At some station a short distance from the town to be entered the wagon may be uncoupled from the train, and a sufficient number of soldiers accompanying the officers will unload the airship and its appliances, transport the whole to the nearest open space, and at once begin inflating the balloon. Within two hours from quitting the train the airship may be ready for its flight to the interior of the technically-besieged town.

'Such may be the outline of the task—a task presented imperiously to French balloonists by the events of 1870-1, and which all the devotion and science of the Tissandier brothers failed to accomplish. To-day the problem may be set with better hope of success. All the essential difficulties may be revived by the marking out of a hostile zone around the town that must be entered; from beyond the outer edge of this zone, then, the airship will rise and take its flight—across it.

'Will the airship be able to rise out of rifle range? I have always been the first to insist that the normal place of the airship is in low altitudes, and I shall have written this book to little purpose if I have not shown the reader the real dangers attending any brusque vertical mounting to considerable heights. For this we have the terrible Severo accident before our eyes. In particular, I have expressed astonishment at hearing of experimenters rising to these altitudes without adequate purpose in their early stages of experience with dirigible balloons. All this is very different, however, from a reasoned, cautious mounting, whose necessity has been foreseen and prepared for.'

Probably owing to the fact that his engines were not of sufficient power, Santos-Dumont cannot be said to have solved the problem of the military airship, although the French Government bought one of his vessels. At the same time, he accomplished much in furthering and inciting experiment with dirigible airships, and he will always rank high among the pioneers of aerostation. His experiments might have gone further had not the Wright brothers' success in America and French interest in the problem of the heavier-than-air machine turned him from the study of dirigibles to that of the aeroplane, in which also he takes high rank among the pioneers, leaving the construction of a successful military dirigible to such men as the Lebaudy brothers, Major Parseval, and Zeppelin.

IV
THE MILITARY DIRIGIBLE

Although French and German experiment in connection with the production of an airship which should be suitable for military purposes proceeded side by side, it is necessary to outline the development in the two countries separately, owing to the differing character of the work carried out. So far as France is concerned, experiment began with the Lebaudy brothers, originally sugar refiners, who turned their energies to airship construction in 1899. Three years of work went to the production of their first vessel, which was launched in 1902, having been constructed by them together with a balloon manufacturer named Surcouf and an engineer, Julliot. The Lebaudy airships were what is known as semi-rigids, having a spar which ran practically the full length of the gas bag to which it was attached in such a way as to distribute the load evenly. The car was suspended from the spar, at the rear end of which both horizontal and vertical rudders were fixed, whilst stabilising fins were provided at the stern of the gas envelope itself. The first of the Lebaudy vessels was named the 'Jaune'; its length was 183 feet and its maximum diameter 30 feet, while the cubic capacity was 80,000 feet. The power unit was a 40 horse-power Daimler motor, driving two propellers and giving a maximum speed of 26 miles per hour. This vessel made 29 trips, the last of which took place in November, 1902, when the airship was wrecked through collision with a tree.

The second airship of Lebaudy construction was 7 feet longer than the first, and had a capacity of 94,000 cubic feet of gas with a triple air bag of 17,500 cubic feet to compensate for loss of gas; this latter was kept inflated by a rotary fan. The vessel was eventually taken over by the French Government and may be counted the first dirigible airship considered fit on its tests for military service.

Later vessels of the Lebaudy type were the 'Patrie' and 'Republique,' in which both size and method of construction surpassed those of the two first attempts. The 'Patrie' was fitted with a 60 horse-power engine which gave a speed of 28 miles an hour, while the vessel had a radius of 280 miles, carrying a crew of nine. In the winter of 1907 the 'Patrie' was anchored at Verdun, and encountered a gale which broke her hold on her mooring-ropes. She drifted derelict westward across France, the Channel, and the British Isles, and was lost in the Atlantic.

The 'Republique' had an 80 horse-power motor, which, however, only gave her the same speed as the 'Patrie.' She was launched in July, 1908, and within three months came to an end which constituted a tragedy for France. A propeller burst while the vessel was in the air, and one blade, flying toward the envelope, tore in it a great gash; the airship crashed to earth, and the two officers and two non-commissioned officers who were in the car were instantaneously killed.

The Clement Bayard, and subsequently the Astra-Torres, non-rigids, followed on the early Lebaudys and carried French dirigible construction up to 1912. The Clement Bayard was a simple non-rigid having four lobes at the stern end to assist stability. These were found to retard the speed of the airship, which in the second and more successful construction was driven by a Clement Bayard motor of 100 horse-power at a speed of 30 miles an hour. On August 23rd, 1909, while being tried for acceptance by the military authorities, this vessel achieved a record by flying at a height of 5,000 feet for two hours. The Astra-Torres non-rigids were designed by a Spaniard, Senor Torres, and built by the Astra Company. The envelope was of trefoil shape, this being due to the interior rigging from the suspension band; the exterior appearance is that of two lobes side by side, overlaid by a third. The interior rigging, which was adopted with a view to decreasing air resistance, supports a low-hung car from the centre of the envelope; steering is accomplished by means of horizontal planes fixed on the envelope at the stern, and vertical planes depending beneath the envelope, also at the stern end.

One of the most successful of French pre-war dirigibles was a Clement Bayard built in 1912. In this twin propellers were placed at the front and horizontal and vertical rudders in a sort of box formation under the envelope at the stern. The envelope was stream-lined, while the car of the machine was placed well forward with horizontal controlling planes above it and immediately behind the propellers. This airship, which was named 'Dupuy de Lome,' may be ranked as about the most successful non-rigid dirigible constructed prior to the War.

Experiments with non-rigids in Germany was mainly carried on by Major Parseval, who produced his first vessel in 1906. The main feature of this airship consisted in variation in length of the suspension cables at the will of the operator, so that the envelope could be given an upward tilt while the car remained horizontal in order to give the vessel greater efficiency in climbing. In this machine, the propeller was placed above and forward of the car, and the controlling planes were fixed directly to the envelope near the forward end. A second vessel differed from the first mainly in the matter of its larger size, variable suspension being again employed, together with a similar method of control. The vessel was moderately successful, and under Major Parseval's direction a third was constructed for passenger carrying, with two engines of 120 horsepower, each driving propellers of 13 feet diameter. This was the most successful of the early German dirigibles; it made a number of voyages with a dozen passengers in addition to its crew, as well as proving its value for military purposes by use as a scout machine in manoeuvres. Later Parsevals were constructed of stream-line form, about 300 feet in length, and with engines sufficiently powerful to give them speeds up to 50 miles an hour.

Major Von Gross, commander of a Balloon Battalion, produced semi-rigid dirigibles from 1907 onward. The second of these, driven by two 75 horse-power Daimler motors, was capable of a speed of 27 miles an hour; in September of 1908 she made a trip from and back to Berlin which lasted 13 hours, in which period she covered 176 miles with four passengers and reached a height of 4,000 feet. Her successor, launched in April of 1909, carried a wireless installation, and the next to this, driven by four motors of 75 horse-power each, reached a speed of 45 miles an hour. As this vessel was constructed for military purposes, very few details either of its speed or method of construction were made public.

Practically all these vessels were discounted by the work of Ferdinand von Zeppelin, who set out from the first with the idea of constructing a rigid dirigible. Beginning in 1898, he built a balloon on an aluminium framework covered with linen and silk, and divided into interior compartments holding linen bags which were capable of containing nearly 400,000 cubic feet of hydrogen. The total length of this first Zeppelin airship was 420 feet and the diameter 38 feet. Two cars were rigidly attached to the envelope, each carrying a 16 horse-power motor, driving propellers which were rigidly connected to the aluminium framework of the balloon. Vertical and horizontal screws were used for lifting and forward driving and a sliding weight was used to raise or lower the stem of the vessel out of the horizontal in order to rise or descend without altering the load by loss of ballast or the lift by loss of gas.

The first trial of this vessel was made in July of 1900, and was singularly unfortunate. The winch by which the sliding weight was operated broke, and the balloon was so bent that the working of the propellers was interfered with, as was the steering. A speed of 13 feet per second was attained, but on descending, the airship ran against some piles and was further damaged. Repairs were completed by the end of September, 1900, and on a second trial flight made on October 21st a speed of 30 feet per second was reached.

Zeppelin was far from satisfied with the performance of this vessel, and he therefore set about collecting funds for the construction of a second, which was completed in 1905. By this time the internal combustion engine had been greatly improved, and without any increase of weight, Zeppelin was able to instal two motors of 85 horse-power each. The total capacity was 367,000 cubic feet of hydrogen, carried in 16 gas bags inside the framework, and the weight of the whole construction was 9 tons—a ton less than that of the first Zeppelin airship. Three vertical planes at front and rear controlled horizontal steering, while rise and fall was controlled by horizontal planes arranged in box form. Accident attended the first trial of this second airship, which took place over the Bodensee on November 30th, 1905, 'It had been intended to tow the raft, to which it was anchored, further from the shore against the wind. But the water was too low to allow the use of the raft. The balloon was therefore mounted on pontoons, pulled out into the lake, and taken in tow by a motor-boat. It was caught by a strong wind which was blowing from the shore, and driven ahead at such a rate that it overtook the motor-boat. The tow rope was therefore at once cut, but it unexpectedly formed into knots and became entangled with the airship, pulling the front end down into the water. The balloon was then caught by the wind and lifted into the air, when the propellers were set in motion. The front end was at this instant pointing in a downward direction, and consequently it shot into the water, where it was found necessary to open the valves.'[*]

[*] Hildebrandt, Airships Past and Present.

The damage done was repaired within six weeks, and the second trial was made on January 17th, 1906. The lifting force was too great for the weight, and the dirigible jumped immediately to 1,500 feet. The propellers were started, and the dirigible brought to a lower level, when it was found possible to drive against the wind. The steering arrangements were found too sensitive, and the motors were stopped, when the vessel was carried by the wind until it was over land—it had been intended that the trial should be completed over water. A descent was successfully accomplished and the dirigible was anchored for the night, but a gale caused it so much damage that it had to be broken up. It had achieved a speed of 30 feet per second with the motors developing only 36 horse-power and, gathering from this what speed might have been accomplished with the full 170 horse-power,

Zeppelin set about the construction of No. 3, with which a number of successful voyages were made, proving the value of the type for military purposes.

No. 4 was the most notable of the early Zeppelins, as much on account of its disastrous end as by reason of any superior merit in comparison with No. 3. The main innovation consisted in attaching a triangular keel to the under side of the envelope, with two gaps beneath which the cars were suspended. Two Daimler Mercedes motors of 110 horse-power each were placed one in each car, and the vessel carried sufficient fuel for a 60-hour cruise with the motors running at full speed. Each motor drove a pair of three-bladed metal propellers rigidly attached to the framework of the envelope and about 15 feet in diameter. There was a vertical rudder at the stern of the envelope and horizontal controlling planes were fixed on the sides of the envelope. The best performances and the end of this dirigible were summarised as follows by Major Squier:—

'Its best performances were two long trips performed during the summer of 1908. The first, on July 4th, lasted exactly 12 hours, during which time it covered a distance of 235 miles, crossing the mountains to Lucerne and Zurich, and returning to the balloon-house near Friedrichshafen, on Lake Constance. The average speed on this trip was 32 miles per hour. On August 4th, this airship attempted a 24-hour flight, which was one of the requirements made for its acceptance by the Government. It left Friedrichshafen in the morning with the intention of following the Rhine as far as Mainz, and then returning to its starting-point, straight across the country. A stop of 3 hours 30 minutes was made in the afternoon of the first day on the Rhine, to repair the engine. On the return, a second stop was found necessary near Stuttgart, due to difficulties with the motors, and some loss of gas. While anchored to the ground, a storm arose which broke loose the anchorage, and, as the balloon rose in the air, it exploded and took fire (due to causes which have never been actually determined and published) and fell to the ground, where it was completely destroyed. On this journey, which lasted in all 31 hours 15 minutes, the airship was in the air 20 hours 45 minutes, and covered a total distance of 378 miles.

'The patriotism of the German nation was aroused. Subscriptions were immediately started, and in a short space of time a quarter of a million pounds had been raised. A Zeppelin Society was formed to direct the expenditure of this fund. Seventeen thousand pounds has been expended in purchasing land near Friedrichshafen; workshops were erected, and it was announced that within one year the construction of eight airships of the Zeppelin type would be completed. Since the disaster to 'Zeppelin IV.' the Crown Prince of Germany made a trip in 'Zeppelin No. 3,' which had been called back into service, and within a very few days the German Emperor visited Friedrichshafen for the purpose of seeing the airship in flight. He decorated Count Zeppelin with the order of the Black Eagle. German patriotism and enthusiasm has gone further, and the "German Association for an Aerial Fleet" has been organised in sections throughout the country. It announces its intention of building 50 garages (hangars) for housing airships.'

By January of 1909, with well over a quarter of a million in hand for the construction of Zeppelin airships, No. 3 was again brought out, probably in order to maintain public enthusiasm in respect of the possible new engine of war. In March of that year No. 3 made a voyage which lasted for 4 hours over and in the vicinity of Lake Constance; it carried 26 passengers for a distance of nearly 150 miles.

Before the end of March, Count Zeppelin determined to voyage from Friedrichshafen to Munich, together with the crew of the airship and four military officers. Starting at four in the morning and ascertaining their route from the lights of railway stations and the ringing of bells in the towns passed over, the journey was completed by nine o'clock, but a strong south-west gale prevented the intended landing. The airship was driven before the wind until three o'clock in the afternoon, when it landed safely near Dingolfing; by the next morning the wind had fallen considerably and the airship returned to Munich and landed on the parade ground as originally intended. At about 3.30 in the afternoon, the homeward journey was begun, Friedrichshafen being reached at about 7.30.

These trials demonstrated that sufficient progress had been made to justify the construction of Zeppelin airships for use with the German army. No. 3 had been manoeuvred safely if not successfully in half a gale of wind, and henceforth it was known as 'SMS. Zeppelin I.,' at the bidding of the German Emperor, while the construction of 'SMS. Zeppelin II.' was rapidly proceeded with. The fifth construction of Count Zeppelin's was 446 feet in length, 42 1/2 feet in diameter, and contained 530,000 cubic feet of hydrogen gas in 17 separate compartments. Trial flights were made on the 26th May, 1909, and a week later she made a record voyage of 940 miles, the route being from Lake Constance over Ulm, Nuremberg, Leipzig, Bitterfeld, Weimar, Heilbronn, and Stuttgart, descending near Goppingen; the time occupied in the flight was upwards of 38 hours.

In landing, the airship collided with a pear-tree, which damaged the bows and tore open two sections of the envelope, but repairs on the spot enabled the return journey to Friedrichshafen to be begun 24 hours later. In spite of the mishap the Zeppelin had once more proved itself as a possible engine of war, and thenceforth Germany pinned its faith to the dirigible, only developing the aeroplane to such an extent as to keep abreast of other nations. By the outbreak of war, nearly 30 Zeppelins had been constructed; considerably more than half of these were destroyed in various ways, but the experiments carried on with each example of the type permitted of improvements being made. The first fatality occurred in September, 1913, when the fourteenth Zeppelin to be constructed, known as Naval Zeppelin L.1, was wrecked in the North Sea by a sudden storm and her crew of thirteen were drowned. About three weeks after this, Naval Zeppelin L.2, the eighteenth in order of building, exploded in mid-air while manoeuvring over Johannisthal. She was carrying a crew of 25, who were all killed.

By 1912 the success of the Zeppelin type brought imitators. Chief among them was the Schutte-Lanz, a Mannheim firm, which produced a rigid dirigible with a wooden framework, wire braced. This was not a cylinder like the Zeppelin, but reverted to the cigar shape and contained about the same amount of gas as the Zeppelin type. The Schutte-Lanz was made with two gondolas rigidly attached to the envelope in which the gas bags were placed. The method of construction involved greater weight than was the case with the Zeppelin, but the second of these vessels, built with three gondolas containing engines, and a navigating cabin built into the hull of the airship itself, proved quite successful as a naval scout until wrecked on the islands off the coast of Denmark late in 1914. The last Schutte-Lanz to be constructed was used by the Germans for raiding England, and was eventually brought down in flames at Cowley.

V
BRITISH AIRSHIP DESIGN

As was the case with the aeroplane, Great Britain left France and Germany to make the running in the early days of airship construction; the balloon section of the Royal Engineers was compelled to confine its energies to work with balloons pure and simple until well after the twentieth century had dawned, and such experiments as were made in England were done by private initiative. As far back as 1900 Doctor Barton built an airship at the Alexandra Palace and voyaged across London in it. Four years later Mr E. T. Willows of Cardiff produced the first successful British dirigible, a semi-rigid 74 feet in length and 18 feet in diameter, engined with a 7 horse-power Peugot twin-cylindered motor. This drove a two-bladed propeller at the stern for propulsion, and also actuated a pair of auxiliary propellers at the front which could be varied in their direction so as to control the right and left movements of the airship. This device was patented and the patent was taken over by the British Government, which by 1908 found Mr Willow's work of sufficient interest to regard it as furnishing data for experiment at the balloon factory at Farnborough. In 1909, Willows steered one of his dirigibles to London from Cardiff in a little less than ten hours, making an average speed of over 14 miles an hour. The best speed accomplished was probably considerably greater than this, for at intervals of a few miles, Willows descended near the earth to ascertain his whereabouts with the help of a megaphone. It must be added that he carried a compass in addition to his megaphone. He set out for Paris in November of 1910, reached the French coast, and landed near Douai. Some damage was sustained in this landing, but, after repair, the trip to Paris was completed.

Meanwhile the Government balloon factory at Farnborough began airship construction in 1907; Colonel Capper, R.E., and S. F. Cody were jointly concerned in the production of a semi-rigid. Fifteen thicknesses of goldbeaters' skin—about the most expensive covering obtainable—were used for the envelope, which was 25 feet in diameter. A slight shower of rain in which the airship was caught led to its wreckage, owing to the absorbent quality of the goldbeaters' skin, whereupon Capper and Cody set to work to reproduce the airship and its defects on a larger scale. The first had been named 'Nulli Secundus' and the second was named 'Nulli Secundus II.' Punch very appropriately suggested that the first vessel ought to have been named 'Nulli Primus,' while a possible third should be christened 'Nulli Tertius.' 'Nulli Secundus II.' was fitted with a 100 horse-power engine and had an envelope of 42 feet in diameter, the goldbeaters' skin being covered in fabric and the car being suspended by four bands which encircled the balloon envelope. In October of 1907, 'Nulli Secundus II.' made a trial flight from Farnborough to London and was anchored at the Crystal Palace. The wind sprung up and took the vessel away from its mooring ropes, wrecking it after the one flight.

Stagnation followed until early in 1909, when a small airship fitted with two 12 horse-power motors and named the 'Baby' was turned out from the balloon factory. This was almost egg-shaped, the blunt end being forward, and three inflated fins being placed at the tail as control members. A long car with rudder and elevator at its rear-end carried the engines and crew; the 'Baby' made some fairly successful flights and gave a good deal of useful data for the construction of later vessels.

Next to this was 'Army Airship 2A 'launched early in 1910 and larger, longer, and narrower in design than the Baby. The engine was an 80 horse-power Green motor which drove two pairs of propellers; small inflated control members were fitted at the stern end of the envelope, which was 154 feet in length. The suspended car was 84 feet long, carrying both engines and crew, and the Willows idea of swivelling propellers for governing the direction was used in this vessel. In June of that year a new, small-type dirigible, the 'Beta,' was produced, driven by a 30 horse-power Green engine with which she flew over 3,000 miles. She was the most successful British dirigible constructed up to that time, and her successor, the 'Gamma,' was built on similar lines. The 'Gamma' was a larger vessel, however, produced in 1912, with flat, controlling fins and rudder at the rear end of the envelope, and with the conventional long car suspended at some distance beneath the gas bag. By this time, the mooring mast, carrying a cap of which the concave side fitted over the convex nose of the airship, had been originated. The cap was swivelled, and, when attached to it, an airship was held nose on to the wind, thus reducing by more than half the dangers attendant on mooring dirigibles in the open.

Private subscription under the auspices of the Morning Post got together sufficient funds in 1910 for the purchase of a Lebaudy airship, which was built in France, flown across the Channel, and presented to the Army Airship Fleet. This dirigible was 337 feet long, and was driven by two 135 horse-power Panhard motors, each of which actuated two propellers. The journey from Moisson to Aldershot was completed at a speed of 36 miles an hour, but the airship was damaged while being towed into its shed. On May of the following year, the Lebaudy was brought out for a flight, but, in landing, the guide rope fouled in trees and sheds and brought the airship broadside on to the wind; she was driven into some trees and wrecked to such an exteent that rebuilding was considered an impossibility. A Clement Bayard, bought by the army airship section, became scrap after even less flying than had been accomplished by the Lebaudy.

In April of 1910, the Admiralty determined on a naval air service, and set about the production of rigid airships which should be able to compete with Zeppelins as naval scouts. The construction was entrusted to Vickers, Ltd., who set about the task at their Barrow works and built something which, when tested after a year's work, was found incapable of lifting its own weight. This defect was remedied by a series of alterations, and meanwhile the unofficial title of 'Mayfly' was given to the vessel.

Taken over by the Admiralty before she had passed any flying tests, the 'Mayfly' was brought out on September 24th, 1911, for a trial trip, being towed out from her shed by a tug. When half out from the shed, the envelope was caught by a light cross-wind, and, in spite of the pull from the tug, the great fabric broke in half, nearly drowning the crew, who had to dive in order to get clear of the wreckage.

There was considerable similarity in form, though not in performance, between the Mayfly and the prewar Zeppelin. The former was 510 feet in length, cylindrical in form, with a diameter of 48 feet, and divided into 19 gas-bag compartments. The motive power consisted of two 200 horse-power Wolseley engines. After its failure, the Naval Air Service bought an Astra-Torres airship from France and a Parseval from Germany, both of which proved very useful in the early days of the War, doing patrol work over the Channel before the Blimps came into being.

Early in 1915 the 'Blimp' or 'S.S.' type of coastal airship was evolved in response to the demand for a vessel which could be turned out quickly and in quantities. There was urgent demand, voiced by Lord Fisher, for a type of vessel capable of maintaining anti-submarine patrol off the British coasts, and the first S.S. airships were made by combining a gasbag with the most available type of aeroplane fuselage and engine, and fitting steering gear. The 'Blimp' consisted of a B.E. fuselage with engine and geared-down propeller, and seating for pilot and observer, attached to an envelope about 150 feet in length. With a speed of between 35 and 40 miles an hour, the 'Blimp' had a cruising capacity of about ten hours; it was fitted with wireless set, camera, machine-gun, and bombs, and for submarine spotting and patrol work generally it proved invaluable, though owing to low engine power and comparatively small size, its uses were restricted to reasonably fair weather. For work farther out at sea and in all weathers, airships known as the coast patrol type, and more commonly as 'coastals,' were built, and later the 'N.S.' or North Sea type, still larger and more weather-worthy, followed. By the time the last year of the War came, Britain led the world in the design of non-rigid and semi-rigid dirigibles. The 'S.S.' or 'Blimp' had been improved to a speed of 50 miles an hour, carrying a crew of three, and the endurance record for the type was 18 1/2 hours, while one of them had reached a height of 10,000 feet. The North Sea type of non-rigid was capable of travelling over 20 hours at full speed, or forty hours at cruising speed, and the number of non-rigids belonging to the British Navy exceeded that of any other country.

It was owing to the incapacity — apparent or real — of the British military or naval designers to produce a satisfactory rigid airship that the 'N.S.' airship was evolved. The first of this type was produced in 1916, and on her trials she was voted an unqualified success, in consequence of which the building of several more was pushed on. The envelope, of 360,000 cubic feet capacity, was made on the Astra-Torres principle of three lobes, giving a trefoil section. The ship carried four fins, to three of which the elevator and rudder flaps were attached; petrol tanks were placed inside the envelope, under which was rigged a long covered-in car, built up of a light steel tubular framework 35 feet in length. The forward portion was covered with duralumin sheeting, an aluminium alloy which, unlike aluminium itself, is not affected by the action of sea air and water, and the remainder with fabric laced to the framework. Windows and port-holes were provided to give light to the crew, and the controls and navigating instruments were placed forward, with the sleeping accommodation aft. The engines were mounted in a power unit structure, separate from the car and connected by wooden gang ways supported by wire cables. A complete electrical installation of two dynamos and batteries for lights, signalling lamps, wireless, telephones, etc., was carried, and the motive power consisted of either two 250 horse-power Rolls-Royce engines or two 240 horse-power Fiat engines. The principal dimensions of this type are length 262 feet, horizontal diameter 56 feet 9 inches, vertical diameter 69 feet 3 inches. The gross lift is 24,300 lbs. and the disposable lift without crew, petrol, oil, and ballast 8,500 lbs. The normal crew carried for patrol work was ten officers and men. This type holds the record of 101 hours continuous flight on patrol duty.

In the matter of rigid design it was not until 1913 that the British Admiralty got over the fact that the 'Mayfly' would not, and decided on a further attempt at the construction of a rigid dirigible. The contract for this was signed in March of 1914; work was suspended in the following February and begun again in July, 1915, but it was not until January of 1917 that the ship was finished, while her trials were not completed until March of 1917, when she was taken over by the Admiralty. The details of the construction and trial of this vessel, known as 'No. 9,' go to show that she did not quite fill the contract requirements in respect of disposable lift until a number of alterations had been made. The contract specified that a speed of at least 45 miles per hour was to be attained at full engine power, while a minimum disposable lift of 5 tons was to be available for movable weights, and the airship was to be capable of rising to a height of 2,000 feet. Driven by four Wolseley Maybach engines of 180 horse-power each, the lift of the vessel was not sufficient, so it was decided to remove the two engines in the after car and replace them by a single engine of 250 horsepower. With this the vessel reached the contract speed of 45 miles per hour with a cruising radius of 18 hours, equivalent to 800 miles when the engines were running at full speed. The vessel served admirably as a training airship, for, by the time she was completed, the No. 23 class of rigid airship had come to being, and thus No. 9 was already out of date.

Three of the 23 class were completed by the end of 1917; it was stipulated that they should be built with a speed of at least 55 miles per hour, a minimum disposable lift of 8 tons, and a capability of rising at an average rate of not less than 1,000 feet per minute to a height of 3,000 feet. The motive power consisted of four 250 horse-power Rolls-Royce engines, one in each of the forward and after cars and two in a centre car. Four-bladed propellers were used throughout the ship.

A 23X type followed on the 23 class, but by the time two ships had been completed, this was practically obsolete. The No. 31 class followed the 23X; it was built on Schutte-Lanz lines, 615 feet in length, 66 feet diameter, and a million and a half cubic feet capacity. The hull was similar to the later types of Zeppelin in shape, with a tapering stern and a bluff, rounded bow. Five cars each carrying a 250 horse-power Rolls-Royce engine, driving a single fixed propeller, were fitted, and on her trials R.31 performed well, especially in the matter of speed. But the experiment of constructing in wood in the Schutte-Lanz way adopted with this vessel resulted in failure eventually, and the type was abandoned.

Meanwhile, Germany had been pushing forward Zeppelin design and straining every nerve in the improvement of rigid dirigible construction, until L.33 was evolved; she was generally known as a super-Zeppelin, and on September 24th, 1916, six weeks after her launching, she was damaged by gun-fire in a raid over London, being eventually compelled to come to earth at Little Wigborough in Essex. The crew gave themselves up after having set fire to the ship, and though the fabric was totally destroyed, the structure of the hull remained intact, so that just as Germany was able to evolve the Gotha bomber from the Handley-Page delivered at Lille, British naval constructors were able to evolve the R.33 type of airship from the Zeppelin framework delivered at Little Wigborough. Two vessels, R.33 and R.34, were laid down for completion; three others were also put down for construction, but, while R.33 and R.34 were built almost entirely from the data gathered from the wrecked L.33, the three later vessels embody more modern design, including a number of improvements, and more especially greater disposable lift. It has been commented that while the British authorities were building R.33 and R.34, Germany constructed 30 Zeppelins on 4 slips, for which reason it may be reckoned a matter for congratulation that the rigid airship did not decide the fate of the War. The following particulars of construction of the R.33 and R.34 types are as given by Major Whale in his survey of British Airships:—

'In all its main features the hull structure of R.33 and R.34 follows the design of the wrecked German Zeppelin airship L.33. 'The hull follows more nearly a true stream-line shape than in the previous ships constructed of duralumin, in which a greater proportion of the greater length was parallel-sided. The Germans adopted this new shape from the Schutte-Lanz design and have not departed from this practice. This consists of a short, parallel body with a long, rounded bow and a long tapering stem culminating in a point. The overall length of the ship is 643 feet with a diameter of 79 feet and an extreme height of 92 feet.

'The type of girders in this class has been much altered from those in previous ships. The hull is fitted with an internal triangular keel throughout practically the entire length. This forms the main corridor of the ship, and is fitted with a footway down the centre for its entire length. It contains water ballast and petrol tanks, bomb storage and crew accommodation, and the various control wires, petrol pipes, and electric leads are carried along the lower part.

'Throughout this internal corridor runs a bridge girder, from which the petrol and water ballast tanks are supported. These tanks are so arranged that they can be dropped clear of the ship. Amidships is the cabin space with sufficient room for a crew of twenty-five. Hammocks can be swung from the bridge girder before mentioned.

'In accordance with the latest Zeppelin practice, monoplane rudders and elevators are fitted to the horizontal and vertical fins.

'The ship is supported in the air by nineteen gas bags, which give a total capacity of approximately two million cubic feet of gas. The gross lift works out at approximately 59 1/2 tons, of which the total fixed weight is 33 tons, giving a disposable lift of 26 1/2 tons.

'The arrangement of cars is as follows: At the forward end the control car is slung, which contains all navigating instruments and the various controls. Adjoining this is the wireless cabin, which is also fitted for wireless telephony. Immediately aft of this is the forward power car containing one engine, which gives the appearance that the whole is one large car.

'Amidships are two wing cars, each containing a single engine. These are small and just accommodate the engines with sufficient room for mechanics to attend to them. Further aft is another larger car which contains an auxiliary control position and two engines.

'It will thus be seen that five engines are installed in the ship; these are all of the same type and horsepower, namely, 250 horse-power Sunbeam. R.33 was constructed by Messrs Armstrong, Whitworth, Ltd.; while her sister ship R.34 was built by Messrs Beardmore on the Clyde.'

Of the two vessels, R.34 appeared rather more airworthy than her sister ship; the lift of the ship justified the carrying of a greater quantity of fuel than had been provided for, and, as she was considered suitable for making a Transatlantic crossing, extra petrol tanks were fitted in the hull and a new type of outer cover was fitted with a view to her making the Atlantic crossing. She made a 21-hour cruise over the North of England and the South of Scotland at the end of May, 1919, and subsequently went for a longer cruise over Denmark, the Baltic, and the north coast of Germany, remaining in the air for 56 hours in spite of very bad weather conditions. Finally, July 2nd was selected as the starting date for the cross Atlantic flight; the vessel was commanded by Major G. H. Scott, A.F.C., with Captain G. S. Greenland as first officer, Second-Lieut. H. F. Luck as second officer, and Lieut. J. D. Shotter as engineer officer. There were also on board Brig.-Gen. E. P. Maitland, representing the Air Ministry, Major J. E. M. Pritchard, representing the Admiralty, and Lieut.-Col. W. H. Hemsley of the Army Aviation Department. In addition to eight tons of petrol, R.34 carried a total number of 30 persons from East Fortune to Long Island, N.Y.

There being no shed in America capable of accommodating the airship, she had to be moored in the open for refilling with fuel and gas, and to make the return journey almost immediately.

Brig.-Gen. Maitland's account of the flight, in itself a record as interesting as valuable, divides the outward journey into two main stages, the first from East Fortune to Trinity Bay, Newfoundland, a distance of 2,050 sea miles, and the second and more difficult stage to Mineola Field, Long Island, 1,080 sea miles. An easy journey was experienced until Newfoundland was reached, but then storms and electrical disturbances rendered it necessary to alter the course, in consequence of which petrol began to run short. Head winds rendered the shortage still more acute, and on Saturday, July 5th, a wireless signal was sent out asking for destroyers to stand by to tow. However, after an anxious night, R.33 landed safely at Mineola Field at 9.55 a.m. on July 6th, having accomplished the journey in 108 hours 12 minutes.

She remained at Mineola until midnight of July 9th, when, although it had been intended that a start should be made by daylight for the benefit of New York spectators, an approaching storm caused preparations to be advanced for immediate departure. She set out at 5.57 a.m. by British summer time, and flew over New York in the full glare of hundreds of searchlights before heading out over the Atlantic. A following wind assisted the return voyage, and on July 13th, at 7.57 a.m., R.34 anchored at Pulham, Norfolk, having made the return journey in 75 hours 3 minutes, and proved the suitability of the dirigible for Transatlantic commercial work. R.80, launched on July 19th, 1920, afforded further proof, if this were needed.

It is to be noted that nearly all the disasters to airships have been caused by launching and landing—the type is safe enough in the air, under its own power, but its bulk renders it unwieldy for ground handling. The German system of handling Zeppelins in and out of their sheds is, so far, the best devised: this consists of heavy trucks running on rails through the sheds and out at either end; on descending, the trucks are run out, and the airship is securely attached to them outside the shed; the trucks are then run back into the shed, taking the airship with them, and preventing any possibility of the wind driving the envelope against the side of the shed before it is safely housed; the reverse process is adopted in launching, which is thus rendered as simple as it is safe.

THE AIRSHIP COMMERCIALLY

Prior to the war period, between the years 1910 and 1914, a German undertaking called the Deutsche Luftfahrt Actien Gesellschaft conducted a commercial Zeppelin service in which four airships known as the Sachsan, Hansa, Victoria Louise, and Schwaben were used. During the four years of its work, the company carried over 17,000 passengers, and over 100,000 miles were flown without incurring one fatality and with only minor and unavoidable accidents to the vessels composing the service. Although a number of English notabilities made voyages in these airships, the success of this only experiment in commercial aerostation seems to have been forgotten since the war. There was beyond doubt a military aim in this apparently peaceful use of Zeppelin airships; it is past question now that all Germany's mechanical development in respect of land sea, and air transport in the years immediately preceding the war, was accomplished with the ulterior aim of military conquest, but, at the same time, the running of this service afforded proof of the possibility of establishing a dirigible service for peaceful ends, and afforded proof too, of the value of the dirigible as a vessel of purely commercial utility.

In considering the possibility of a commercial dirigible service, it is necessary always to bear in mind the disadvantages of first cost and upkeep as compared with the aeroplane. The building of a modern rigid is an exceedingly costly undertaking, and the provision of an efficient supply of hydrogen gas to keep its compartments filled is a very large item in upkeep of which the heavier-than-air machine goes free. Yet the future of commercial aeronautics so far would seem to lie with the dirigible where very long voyages are in question. No matter how the aeroplane may be improved, the possibility of engine failure always remains as a danger for work over water. In seaplane or flying boat form, the danger is still present in a rough sea, though in the American Transatlantic flight, N.C.3, taxi-ing 300 miles to the Azores after having fallen to the water, proved that this danger is not so acute as is generally assumed. Yet the multiple-engined rigid, as R.34 showed on her return voyage, may have part of her power plant put out of action altogether and still complete her voyage very successfully, which, in the case of mail carrying and services run strictly to time, gives her an enormous advantage over the heavier-than-air machine.

'For commercial purposes,' General Sykes has remarked, 'the airship is eminently adapted for long distance journeys involving non-stop flights. It has this inherent advantage over the aeroplane, that while there appears to be a limit to the range of the aeroplane as at present constructed, there is practically no limit whatever to that of the airship, as this can be overcome by merely increasing the size. It thus appears that for such journeys as crossing the Atlantic, or crossing the Pacific from the west coast of America to Australia or Japan, the airship will be peculiarly suitable. It having been conceded that the scope of the airship is long distance travel, the only type which need be considered for this purpose is the rigid. The rigid airship is still in an embryonic state, but sufficient has already been accomplished in this country, and more particularly in Germany, to show that with increased capacity there is no reason why, within a few years' time, airships should not be built capable of completing the circuit of the globe and of conveying sufficient passengers and merchandise to render such an undertaking a paying proposition.'

The British R.38 class, embodying the latest improvements in airship design outside Germany, gives a gross lift per airship of 85 tons and a net lift of about 45 tons. The capacity of the gas bags is about two and three-quarter million cubic feet, and, travelling at the rate of 45 miles per hour, the cruising range of the vessel is estimated at 8.8 days. Six engines, each of 350 horse-power, admit of an extreme speed of 70 miles per hour if necessary.

The last word in German design is exemplified in the rigids L.70 and L.71, together with the commercial airship 'Bodensee.' Previous to the construction of these, the L.65 type is noteworthy as being the first Zeppelin in which direct drive of the propeller was introduced, together with an improved and lighter type of car. L.70 built in 1918 and destroyed by the British naval forces, had a speed of about 75 miles per hour; L.71 had a maximum speed of 72 miles per hour, a gas bag capacity of 2,420,000 cubic feet, and a length of 743 feet, while the total lift was 73 tons. Progress in design is best shown by the progress in useful load; in the L.70 and L.71 class, this has been increased to 58.3 per cent, while in the Bodensee it was ever higher.

As was shown in R.34's American flight, the main problem in connection with the commercial use of dirigibles is that of mooring in the open. The nearest to a solution of this problem, so far, consists in the mast carrying a swivelling cap; this has been tried in the British service with a non-rigid airship, which was attached to a mast in open country in a gale of 52 miles an hour without the slightest damage to the airship. In its commercial form, the mast would probably take the form of a tower, at the top of which the cap would revolve so that the airship should always face the wind, the tower being used for embarkation and disembarkation of passengers and the provision of fuel and gas. Such a system would render sheds unnecessary except in case of repairs, and would enormously decrease the establishment charges of any commercial airship.

All this, however, is hypothetical. Remains the airship of to-day, developed far beyond the promise of five years ago, capable, as has been proved by its achievements both in Britain and in Germany, of undertaking practically any given voyage with success.

VII
KITE BALLOONS

As far back as the period of the Napoleonic wars, the balloon was given a place in warfare, but up to the Franco-Prussian Prussian War of 1870-71 its use was intermittent. The Federal forces made use of balloons to a small extent in the American Civil War; they came to great prominence in the siege of Paris, carrying out upwards of three million letters and sundry carrier pigeons which took back messages into the besieged city. Meanwhile, as captive balloons, the German and other armies used them for observation and the direction of artillery fire. In this work the ordinary spherical balloon was at a grave disadvantage; if a gust of wind struck it, the balloon was blown downward and down wind, generally twirling in the air and upsetting any calculations and estimates that might be made by the observers, while in a wind of 25 miles an hour it could not rise at all. The rotatory movement caused by wind was stopped by an experimenter in the Russo-Japanese war, who fixed to the captive observation balloons a fin which acted as a rudder. This did not stop the balloon from being blown downward and away from its mooring station, but this tendency was overcome by a modification designed in Germany by the Parseval-Siegsfield Company, which originated what has since become familiar as the 'Sausage' or kite balloon. This is so arranged that the forward end is tilted up into the wind, and the underside of the gas bag, acting as a plane, gives the balloon a lifting tendency in a wind, thus counteracting the tendency of the wind to blow it downward and away from its mooring station. Smaller bags are fitted at the lower and rear end of the balloon with openings that face into the wind; these are thus kept inflated, and they serve the purpose of a rudder, keeping the kite balloon steady in the air.

Various types of kite balloon have been introduced; the original German Parseval-Siegsfield had a single air bag at the stern end, which was modified to two, three, or more lobes in later varieties, while an American experimental design attempted to do away with the attached lobes altogether by stringing out a series of small air bags, kite fashion, in rear of the main envelope. At the beginning of the War, Germany alone had kite balloons, for the authorities of the Allied armies con-sidered that the bulk of such a vessel rendered it too conspicuous a mark to permit of its being serviceable. The Belgian arm alone possessed two which, on being put into service, were found extremely useful. The French followed by constructing kite balloons at Chalais Meudon, and then, after some months of hostilities and with the example of the Royal Naval Air Service to encourage them, the British military authorities finally took up the construction and use of kite balloons for artillery-spotting and general observation purposes. Although many were brought down by gun-fire, their uses far outweighed their disadvantages, and toward the end of the War, hardly a mile of front was without its 'Sausage.'

For naval work, kite balloons were carried in a specially constructed hold in the forepart of certain vessels; when required for use, the covering of the hold was removed, the kite balloon inflated and released to the required height by means of winches as in the case of the land work. The perfecting of the 'Coastal' and N.S. types of airship, together with the extension of wireless telephony between airship and cruiser or other warship, in all probability will render the use of the kite balloon unnecessary in connection with naval scouting. But, during the War, neither wireless telephony nor naval airships had developed sufficiently to render the Navy independent of any means that might come to hand, and the fitting of kite balloons in this fashion filled a need of the times.

A necessary accessory of the kite balloon is the parachute, which has a long history. Da Vinci and Veranzio appear to have been the first exponents, the first in the theory and the latter in the practice of parachuting. Montgolfier experimented at Annonay before he constructed his first hot air-balloon, and in 1783 a certain Lenormand dropped from a tree in a parachute. Blanchard the balloonist made a spectacle of parachuting, and made it a financial success; Cocking, in 1836, attempted to use an inverted form of parachute; taken up to a height of 3,000 feet, he was cut adrift, when the framework of the parachute collapsed and Cocking was killed.

The rate of fall is slow in parachuting to the ground. Frau Poitevin, making a descent from a height of 6,000 feet, took 45 minutes to reach the ground, and, when she alighted, her husband, who had taken her up, had nearly got his balloon packed up. Robertson, another parachutist is said to have descended from a height of 10,000 feet in 35 minutes, or at a rate of nearly 5 feet per second. During the War Brigadier-General Maitland made a parachute descent from a height of 10,000 feet, the time taken being about 20 minutes.

The parachute was developed considerably during the War period, the main requirement, that of certainty in opening, being considerably developed. Considered a necessary accessory for kite balloons, the parachute was also partially adopted for use with aeroplanes in the later War period, when it was contended that if a machine were shot down in flames, its occupants would be given a far better chance of escape if they had parachutes. Various trials were made to demonstrate the extreme efficiency of the parachute in modern form, one of them being a descent from the upper ways of the Tower Bridge to the waters of the Thames, in which short distance the 'Guardian Angel' type of parachute opened and cushioned the descent for its user.

For dirigibles, balloons, and kite balloons the parachute is an essential. It would seem to be equally essential in the case of heavier-than-air machines, but this point is still debated. Certainly it affords the occupant of a falling aeroplane a chance, no matter how slender, of reaching the ground in safety, and, for that reason, it would seem to have a place in aviation as well as in aerostation.